FURNACE BROOK

Collected Poems

By

Frederick Pheiffer

ISBN: 0-75964-604-X

Library of Congress Control Number: 2001118074

This book is printed on acid free paper.

1stBooks – rev. 7/3/01

Dedicated to the memory
of my father
John H. Pheiffer

And

Edward J. McBride
mentor and friend

The author wishes to thank
Maryellen Hedderman
for her helpful suggestions
and copyediting

Without memory there's no continuity
...the way I see time is that all the things
that have ever occurred in my life are
always present in my life, the past is never
excluded from the present...

David Kherdian
Poet

CONTENTS

I

Furnace Brook

Frederick Pheiffer

FURNACE BROOK

For hundreds of years
the brook has meandered
through the rolling hills of
Oxford, New Jersey.

Deposits of iron ore lay
beneath the fields and hills
until immigrants came to this place
to work the mines.

Early in the 1700's, the hills of
Oxford were named: Dutch Hill,
Mine Hill, Cat Swamp, Tunnel Hill,
Rattlesnake Hill, and Van Nest Hill.

Oxford Furnace was built in 1741
near the churning waters.

Settlers came and the native
Leni Lenape Indians left.
Their way of life replaced by the fires
stoked to melt ore into iron.

Today, only shadows remain
of the furnace ruins.
No marker will ever tell the story of the
men who worked and died here.
There are no tributes to the

Frederick Pheiffer

Leni Lenapes who died in exile.

**Only Furnace Brook continues
its unending journey
through these silent hills.**

OXFORD
NEW JERSEY

Oxford had a post office,
Louie Steinhardt's
shoe store, Doc. Reuther's
drugstore, and Oram's
grocery store.

Harry Wilkenson pumped a
a dollars worth of gas.
Across the street was Fictels
ice cream and candy store.
Kinney's barber shop was
next to Frank Cain's
blacksmith shop.
A fire house with one truck.

Furnace Brook flowed through the town.

Churches of all type,
Methodist, Catholic, Presbyterian,
German Lutheran and Dutch Reformed.

In the center of town was
the Yankee factory.
Some of the buildings
still stand,

paint faded like the memories
that will slowly
be forgotten.

It is a long time ago when
all of this was there.

BLACKSMITH

Frank Cain was
the blacksmith
in Oxford.

A solitary man
who labored
at his art.

Hammer and anvil,
he shoed horses
for the farmers,
from red hot beds
of coals,
that seemed to burn
forever.

Frederick Pheiffer

FINNEGAN BROTHERS

Mike and Joe lived alone
in a ramshackle house
on School Street.

They dug graves for a
living and drank at Bosco's
at the end of the day.

Mike and Joe had to walk
past our house to get home.
It was always an effort.
Too much whiskey,
often falling into the ditch.

Brothers leaning on each other,
it was all they had.

Day after day,
they struggled,
sleeping off the drink
only to begin it again
the following day.

ICE TRUCK

Bosco's tavern was at the end of our street.
Blocks of ice were used to chill
the beer at the bar.

Each day, the iceman would stop at Bosco's
taking huge ice blocks into the tavern.
Going back outside,
he would stand at the end
of his truck and grind chunks of ice
into small white mountains.

As soon as he was inside the tavern
we raced to the truck to grab handfuls of ice.
You had to be quick,
if caught,
you had your ears boxed.

These were simple times.
Endless hours in the summer
swinging on the metal railings,
waiting for the ice truck
at Bosco's tavern.

FRANCIS PETTINGER

Oxford Town Librarian,
Miss Pettinger's authority
was never questioned once you
entered the one room library.

Firm jaw, white hair pulled tightly
into a small bun, eye glasses perched
on her nose as she greeted me
each time that I went to the library.

It seemed that each book belonged to her.
I always remember her stern warning
"return the books on time."

The years passed.

Miss Pettinger died alone.
She had lived by herself
in a small house on Dutch Hill,
in Oxford.

Her spirit is still with me.
I remember how she helped me
find "good books" by the armful.

One summer she sponsored
a reading contest.
Prizes were awarded to a girl and boy who read
the most books.

I won the boy's prize- a blue and orange
polka dot bow tie.

Each book I read
brings back her memory.

Frederick Pheiffer

WILLIE GREEN

Willie Green lived on Dutch Hill.
He sold fresh produce
from a truck
filled with fruits
and vegetables.
There were no supermarkets.

When he stopped at our house,
my mother would go outside and
haggle a bit, but Willie always
sold her something.

Willie Green and his truck
are gone just like
the way
we lived.

REUTHER'S
PHARMACY

He was called
Doc Reuther.
Whenever sick
with a cold or in pain,
my mother
would send me to Reuther's
store for a bottle
of Paregoric.
Doc never needed a
prescription.
We paid him
when we could.

There was a small soda fountain
in the rear of his store.
After serving a funeral
mass, I would take the dollar
that the undertaker gave me,
and go to Reuther's
for an ice cream soda,
before returning to school.

Doc and his wife Bessie
lived all their lives
in Oxford.

**They rest forever
in St. Rose of Lima
cemetery, his epitaph
should be:**

**A Good Man
Who Helped The
People Of Oxford**

ST. ROSE OF LIMA

As an altar boy, I served
at the 7a.m. daily mass.

Mrs. Collins laid out the vestments.
I filled the cruets with water
and wine. After lighting
the altar candles, I rang the
bell for mass to begin.

During mass, I learned
Latin by listening to
the words of the priest.

While pouring the water
and wine into the chalice,
I never understood why
Father always needed more wine.

JIMMY DOHNEY

Immigrants from Ireland,
the Dohney family
settled in Oxford.

Jimmy had worked all his
life in Oxford's factories.
When his wife died at
an early age, Jimmy
had no one.

He took to drinking.

Grief was lessened
with each empty bottle.

Day after day, Jimmy
would sit on the bridge
that crossed Furnace Brook
rambling to anyone who would
listen to his lament.

My father tried to help
Jimmy in his struggles,
visiting him on the bridge.

After talking with my father
Jimmy would utter the words
"...this will end, and
over the hills I'll go,
to the poor house
to die."

Frederick Pheiffer

BALTIMORE CATECHISM

Twice a week
we had to go to
church for
religious instruction.
Lessons were taught
by the sisters of St. Joseph.

With the Baltimore Catechism
in one hand
and a ruler in the other,
they taught us that our
faith was based on
fear and guilt.

Slap of the ruler
across my hand,
I would be told "behave,"
"pay attention" when
all that I was doing
was talking to the Lord.

DOCKER'S POND

We walked the railroad tracks,
out through the fields,
to get to the swimming hole.

Racing each other to the water,
clothes thrown off,
we skinny dipped in our
sanctuary.

The boys of Oxford,
relishing the summer days,
unaware how soon
it would all
slip away.

Frederick Pheiffer

PENNY CANDY

Ma and Vic Fictel
sold comics, ice cream sodas,
newspapers and penny candies.

Glass cases
holding trays
of penny sweets.

Ten cent comics that we tried
to read before Ma yelled at us
to buy it or leave.

Ma and Vic are gone, like
the penny candies,
the building is all that remains,
with nothing but memories.

BUTLER PARK

A foot bridge crossed
the brook leading to the
amusement park.

Merry-go-round where you
reached for a metal ring,
the brass one gave you a
free ride.

Bumper cars, swings, pony rides,
and a penny arcade.

Pavillion with bright green
picnic tables next to a field
where our fathers played baseball.

Picnic baskets filled,
hot dogs on the grill.

A day for families,
time away from work.

Frederick Pheiffer

FLEXIBLE FLYER

Snow storm,
school closed,
we took our Flexible Flyers
to Church Street.

Running with our sleds
chest high, we belly-flopped
onto the snow,
tearing down the hill.

Back to the top,
repeat it again,
having so much fun
riding your sled
over the snow.

MRS. BOSCO

Josephine Bosco
made the best
Italian bread in Oxford.

I remember eating
slices with melted butter
and drinking a bottle of soda.

Her kitchen was filled
with smells that were
new to me.

I always found some
excuse to visit her,
knowing that I would
be sent home with a loaf
of her bread,
and the admonition
"mangia- Freddie, eat !"

Frederick Pheiffer

II

From Here To There

Frederick Pheiffer

FROM HERE TO THERE

Shadows reach across the field
until the season's first cutting
is safely put into the barn.

Mountains fill the open sky,
white capped by snows
holding memories of you
left over from seasons past.

Swirling soft breezes
from here,
reminding me
of what was
and what might have been.

Frederick Pheiffer

EVENING TIME

As the sun gives way
to the evening light
a few small stars
appear over us.

Walking out to the
back meadow,
I hold your hand
as we fill our hearts
with the light
from the moon.

AUNT MARGUERITE

Visiting you in the hospital,
I try to tell you
how much
you have meant to me
over the years,
and how much I liked
being with you.

You are alone now,
no children, all your
sisters and brothers
are gone.

Holding your hand,
I show you some
photographs of my sons
as you seem to recognize them.

I whisper to you as you doze,
you are the only one remaining,
please stay
as long as you can,
...you are all that I have.

CAPE COD '89

For the first time in so many years
I went back to the sea.

Vivid memories of you
came to me as I watched the waves
rushing to the shore.

I phoned your cottage
hoping to hear your voice.

When you answered and we spoke,
I knew that we were dusting off
a covered jar of memories,
filled with so much laughter
kept silent for too long.

ENDEARMENT

After meeting you
I soon realized that
you had touched my soul
with the sun's morning light.

Each day brought
unknown energies
flowing into my life.

...and then it ended.

The years have passed.
Now
when I
think of you,
your laughter
comes running back
over paths
we never took.

Frederick Pheiffer

SNOW AND MUSIC

As the young cellist
  walks from the audience
  to his stand
the snow begins to fall.
He and his brother,
  cello and viola,
prepare to play.
The younger nervously tunes
  with the accompanist,
the older calmly waits his turn.

The snow falls silently
  outside
as the music rises
  inside,
giving voice to the soundless
  snowflakes
in their ephemeral fall.

Through the window
  I watch the snow
and listen to the music
  my sons make.
John fills the room with deep
  rich cello tones;
Adam evokes the full
  viola sound.

**I stare at the accompanying
cold white flakes
outside the window
as the music of my sons
warms the soul within.**

Frederick Pheiffer

SCULLING BOAT

Alone on the water
I row
my wooden boat
in the early
morning hours.

The silence is broken
as a blue heron
lifts off the water
flying over me.

Dropping my oars into
the still waters,
I glide into
the enfolding mist.

VERMONT 1

Snow comes so quietly
a white blanket
covering the ground
where once the summer grass
—green, vibrant green—
grew.

This first snow
chooses the old apple tree
covering the branches
where once the autumn leaves
—gold, flame and rust—
hung
bright,
before the soft snow.

VERMONT 2

**Grey cedar shed
empty now,
long memories
held closely together
by weathered shingles
locked in close embrace.**

VERMONT 3

I wake
just before dawn.
The snow is gone
as softly as it arrived,
grey tree lines
silhouetted
against the morning sky.

TOGETHER

You and I
standing here
watching the sun
disappear beyond the sea.

We embrace,
waves dance around us
completing their endless
journey
to the shore.

Waves recede
into the ocean leaving
behind silken sands
for us to begin our life
together.

THE WIND

At the funeral service
for their grandfather,
my sons
could hear the wind
blowing and gusting
outside the church.

Inside, three preachers
were conducting a service
for the man who was being
buried.

My sons held my hands
as the wind intensified.

Leaning over them
I whispered,
"whenever you want
to hear your grandfather
speaking to you
just listen
to the wind."

MONTANA WOMAN

Roots taken from stone
and sky.

Montana's waters and mountains
fill your soul as it awakens
anew with each season.

Steadfast in your journey
you have touched
so many people
with your spirit.

Now in these quiet hours
I reminisce,
realizing that I knew you
long before we met.

AUTUMN

In a field
of wild flowers,
autumn arrives.
The oak drops
its acorns,
giving life
to the earth,
once again.

Frederick Pheiffer

III

Gentle Breezes

Frederick Pheiffer

ONE

A solitary bird
soars among
the clouds
painting
broad strokes
of colors
against the sky.

CELLO

In the passage
with your cello
a power
guides you,
wrapping
a spiritual
shroud
around your music.

Two souls,
inseparable,
the cello
is you.

TURNING THE EARTH

As the horse pulls his plow,
the farmer walks behind,
guiding the blade as it cuts
into the hardened soil
for spring planting.

Man and horse
working together,
in unspoken effort,
as the reins lay gently
on the horse.

Horse and man,
renewing their spirits
each spring,
year after year.

FOREVER

**For just
one moment,
let your heart
be free,
and tell me
that
you love me.**

RIVER

Grey waters
shrouded by curtains
of soft mist that touch
upon the shore.

Wild ducks move quietly
in their own ballet.

Buoy markers bob
back and forth
lighting a pathway.

A small boat
makes its way on the river
in a journey
that was set
in place
long ago.

ENDLESS SKY

The sun's rays
spread out flat
against the sky,
cascading clouds,
breezes gently wrap
around me.

FREEDOM ROW '89

Four empty wheel chairs
left behind on the docks.

Four disabled rowers
sitting in their boats
as they journey
down the Hudson.

Each rower
filled with courage,
as the oars slice into
the water.

Frederick Pheiffer

FROM YOUR HEART

Daily phone calls,
helping me
in my time of pain.

You touched
my soul,
comforting
a weary heart,
as I held onto
your words.

SNOW GEESE

As the snow geese
glide softly down
from the sky,
evening shadows
give way to a field
of white.

Resting from their flight,
sentries are posted
as the flock eats.

At the first light
of dawn
the geese lift off
with joyous sound
flying in set formations.

The field is barren
until their return.

Frederick Pheiffer

IV

A Passage

Frederick Pheiffer

A PASSAGE

A long time ago,
in the foothills of Chenango Valley,
an athlete named Donald McBride
enrolled at Colgate University.

Soon records were set
on Colgate's playing fields.
This lad from Utica excelled in
baseball, football and basketball.
McBride put his numbers on the board
game after game. Varsity letters awarded
for each sport.

In hallowed hallways trophies stand,
a silent tribute to the spirit and soul
of Donald McBride.

Now, another time and another place,
shadows stretch across a different playing field
in Halifax, Nova Scotia.

It is time for Edward McBride's
classroom to fall silent.
For over 25 years, the son of Donald McBride
has been putting his own numbers
on the academic boards at St. Mary's University.

Honored as Professor Emeritus, his feats
will live forever in the hearts of his students.

Professor McBride brought talent and character
into his classroom, leading his students
through the intricacies of learning.

His students' successes
will forever ring loud and clear
in the halls of
St. Mary's University.

Each man, father and son
excelled with valor.

Each man left his
own unique mark of
honor-talent-character.

Professor McBride's students
will always remember
how he changed their lives.
The encouraging touch of his genius,
the goodness of his purpose,
goes on with each of us.

We will never forget
the magic that he gave us.

CONSERVATORY OF MUSIC

Cello resting between his legs
cradled ever so gently,
my son plays his music.

A joyous sound
fills the practice room
as his bow moves across
the cello's strings.

Our eyes meet,
unspoken words are offered.

Once again,
celebrating
our time together.

Frederick Pheiffer

SO LONG AGO

The cardinal's song
wanders through the early
evening quiet.

His serenade reminds
me of a melody
my father sang
each night
just before he read to me.

PROFESSOR BERNER

Raymond Berner
taught English
at a small catholic college
in rural Pennsylvania.

Beginning his lectures
with readings from
James Thurber,
he opened our hearts
with laughter.

Professor Berner
awakened our minds
with his teaching.

Shakespeare, Dante, Keats,
and Thurber danced off the
books' pages
as he lead us through
the maze of learning.

I look back now,
recalling
the excitement
and laughter,
that reverberated
in his classroom.

Frederick Pheiffer

VOUS

**After hours of conversation
with you,
I realized that I had finally
found someone
that I wanted to be
with
the rest of my life.**

SOLO RECITAL

The evening's recital
is over.
Applause ended,
a discarded program
lies on the floor.

The musician sits alone
on the empty stage
thinking about his
performance.

Placing the bow
on his cello,
he begins to play
music from the
evening's recital.

His soothing melody
gives thanks
to the forces
guiding him,
and for filling
his soul
with song.

THE VISIT

Mist floats quietly over the meadow
touching the fresh cut hay.
The early morning sun
warming the ground as the horses
walk into the field.

Suez, Bo, and Pogo.
Two thoroughbreds and a pony
beginning their new lives here among the hills.
Each soul saved from an uncertain end.

On this late summer day, Bo has a visitor.
Adam had trained and raced Bo.

Watching his life's
dream gliding over the track.
Then it ended. Fractured leg.
Surgery and rest.

Months later, Bo raced again.
He pulled up lame
there would be no more races.

Everyone said to put him down,
the horse is "no good anymore,
this is a business."

Bo would have another life.
His friend would only
let him go for adoption.

So on this bright summer morning
old friends meet again
knowing that it was time
to say good bye.

A LETTER

My son's letter
arrived today.

He wrote, "now that I
need your guidance
you are there to help..."

My father received a
similar note from me
a long time ago.

And so it goes,
son to father,
father to son,

generation
to
generation.

NANNA

Born in 1866,
Glasgow, Scotland.

My grandmother immigrated
to America at age eleven,
she traveled alone.

Meeting her parents at Ellis
Island, they settled in
southern New Jersey.

Nanna married and raised
seven children.

I remember sitting on her
lap at age four. She died
in 1944.

All that is left is my one memory
of her holding me.

I now visit Nanna's grave,
leaving flowers,
letting her know that
she is not forgotten.

Frederick Pheiffer

TO LOVE YOU

I had stopped looking,
it all seemed
so hopeless.

All my dreams had been
placed in a box
and put away.

Then, without warning,
you came into my life.
Touching my soul
with gentle words
from your heart.

ADAM PHEIFFER

With your birth,
I began to understand
the meaning of immortality.
You would continue
my family name,
passed on
from the fields
of Ireland,
to the mountains
of Scotland,
and the waters of Hamburg.

This seamless web from
generation to generation,
continues with you.

Frederick Pheiffer

MY FATHER

My father was born
5 November 1900.

Limited education,
he left school to help his family.
My father's first job,
working with his hands
at the Standard Silk Mill
in Phillipsburg, New Jersey.

The earliest memories of my father
were the times we read together
each night.

Supper dishes put away, we sat
together on the couch.
Dad reading to me,
I never wanted the pages to end.

As the years passed
I have never forgotten
my father's passion
for books.

Dad's singular gift to me
was his love for reading.

My father is gone now.
Just before he died,
Dad said to me,
"If I can only find where
the rainbow is... I'll be
alright."

On August 1, 1986,
a
rainbow
was placed
ever so gently
against the sky.

Frederick Pheiffer

V

There Must Be A Reason

Frederick Pheiffer

NURSING HOME

Across the hall
a woman sits
in her chair,
eyes closed
sleep enfolds.

No one visits.

Day after day
her life is repeated
by the same lonely waiting.

POGO

Our beloved pony,
we found you
after you had been saved
from slaughter.

Illnesses and worries came with you.
We tried so hard to save you.
The doctors did everything
to heal you.
Nothing worked.

Today we held your head
for the final time
and kissed
your soft nose
as we said goodbye.

You left us with your heart filled
with love for your journey.

As you roam the fields of gold
may your days be filled with song
as your wonderful mane is
gently touched by the angels.

POGO II

The winter snow storm
lays heavily on the roof
of the horse stalls.

Each day Suez and Bo
walk to visit
Pogo's empty stall.
Bo ignores his pile of hay
as he wistfully stares into the
vacant space waiting for his
little friend to come home.

Leaving the two horses,
I walk out to the back meadow
to visit Pogo's grave.

The morning sun blankets
the field, casting dark shadows off
nearby trees.

Looking across the meadow
an apple tree stands dormant.

**I remember how Pogo and Bo
would race to it
searching for the new apples
that had fallen to the ground.**

It is so quiet now.

SHADOWS DANCING

Drumlins overlapping,
shadows dart out from
the tree tops lined
against the sky.

Darkness covers
the hills,
a star appears
in the sky,
its light falling
on this quiet place.

Two horses glide
about the meadow,
lead by the shadow
of their friend,
Pogo.

IN MEMORIAM

Unaccustomed
we participate in the rituals
of grief.

Friends and family
gather together
in quiet space.

Flowers and cards
cannot replace this
immense loss.

Courage is needed.

We are once again reminded,
that the death
we fear
is our own.

FALLON

Sleeping next to us, your
breathing sooths our spirits.

Remembering how we found
you abandoned in a shelter.

How could anyone have let you go.
We took you away from that place
embracing you with our love.

After a long time
you began to understand
that you had found your
home.

Now, another challenge
a serious illness.

Your brave heart
will give you strength.

All that we ask is that you
not give up,
skilled hands and prayers
will bring you safely home.

BURTON REED
In Memoriam

On a snowy cold day
Burton died.

A rugged man who worked
with his mind and hands
for over eighty years.

He cleared the land and built a home.
The brook was filled with fish,
wild game roamed his woods.

Burton enjoyed a joke and gentle teasing.
He loved without fuss.
His words were plain spoken.

Honest and good
there are not many men that
had his strong moral values.

Somehow we will continue
to hold onto his ways
as we travel into our own future.

ALBANY RURAL CEMETERY

In a small part
of this vast
expanse,
six indigent Scots
are buried.

This sacred burial ground
was created by the
St. Andrew's Society.

We must never forget
the countless immigrants
who came here to America,
especially those who died
alone.

Frederick Pheiffer

ALONE

**I sit at the window,
waiting for you
to come home.**

I miss you so much.

LEAVING

My young son looks at me
with grief shadowed
in his eyes.

His face is etched in pain
as I try to explain
my leaving .

I say to him that I can no longer live
with his mother, our marriage
is over.
My explanations
only create additional confusion.

He can not understand
why I must go.

Running to his favorite
tree in the field,
hiding behind it
my son he calls out
to me
not to leave.

Pleading for words
of comfort
that never come.

PRIEST

After mass today
you told me that you
were leaving the priesthood.

You will always be remembered
for your ministry
and enlightened sermons.

You served your people
with God's love.

Whenever I listen to Verdi's
Four Sacred Pieces
I will think of you.

DOTTIE

Dottie has just died.

Her body was filled
with cancer.

She was a teacher,
a music teacher.
There was no one better.

Devoted to her students,
music became a part
of their lives.

the piano
is silent

Dottie has gone from us
to a place where
angels sing
in joyous praise
to her.

She
has gone
home.

Frederick Pheiffer

AMEN

We assemble at the Police Officers
Memorial.

This sacred place is dedicated to those
brave men and women
who died in the line of duty.

Drums and bagpipes play the
mournful refrains of Amazing Grace.
The music painfully reminds us
of the lives taken from us.

The drum's muffled cadence
reminds us of
oaths taken
in honor's duty.

No speeches, music, or tributes
can bring them back to us.

The marble stone list name after name,
inscribed but never to be forgotten.

The bagpipes final notes drift away
ending with a twenty-one gun salute.

We silently leave these sacred grounds.

MEDALS

Forgotten wars,
remembered only by
those who wear
their medals.

Ceremony, honor,
to be worn with
dignity for service
rendered in battle.

You relive the bullets
tearing through your comrades
as you fought to save others
and to survive.

Does anyone understand
what it meant
to serve
and
die for your
country.

Some of us
will never
forget.

ZACHARY

Son of the earth
your song filled
our hearts with love.

In your spiritual journey
you gave us
a magic that
we will not forget.

Your song gave us music
never heard before and
a poem that ended too soon.

All that we ask
is that you continue singing
as God wraps His arms
around you.

CEMETERY

Here in this flat expanse with
row after row of silent monuments
tributes to the souls
who once lived among us.

On this cold and bleak day,
we have come here to bury one of our own.

A long black hearse leads us
in somber procession.

Family and friends wait
their turn to pay tribute in a ritual
that is repeated hour after hour
day after day in unending repetition.

Eulogies and
prayers are offered,
flowers are placed on the casket.

As we leave this place
a cold air chills us
as snow begins to fall.

Frederick Pheiffer

VI

Assorted Melodies

Frederick Pheiffer

WILLIAMSTOWN

With no words
between them,
two elderly people,
man and woman,
sit side by side
at a picnic table reading
the sunday newspapers.

The only sound,
is the sound
of the pages
being turned.

ROWING

"At the ready,
Row!"

Out go the arms,
curved back follows
hands over legs
up the slide
into the catch.

Legs down
into the drive
hands extended on the oar
as if suspended in the air.
Legs driving
as the oar sweeps
alongside the boat
below the water's surface.

Oars up,
out,
feathered
and squared.

Again.
Arms, backs, legs
legs, backs, arms...
one motion
on each run of the seat.

The dream of rowing
now here
within the boat.

Hour after hour
learning the technique
balancing mind and body
into one
fluid motion.

Something drives you on
through the pain
finding the rhythm,
moving the boat.

Frederick Pheiffer

LILAC

Like my response to the spring flowers,
  you bring gentle feelings
  when I think of you.

Like the heavy fragrance of the lilac,
  my senses are awakened
  when I think of you.

Without words
I hold this precious flower,
  and
I think of you.

QUITTING TIME

My father worked
as a machinist in
Oxford's Yankee
factory.
When his shift ended,
I would walk
to Mine Hill Road.
Sitting on the curb,
I waited for him
to drive up the hill
from work.

When Dad saw me
waiting,
he pulled over and opened
the car door for me
to get in and sit
next to him as we
headed home.

I remember how much
this evening ritual
meant to my
father.

Frederick Pheiffer

SILVER BELL

One small silver bell
found on a dusty shelf
in a nearby antique shop.

As I held the bell
memories of Christmas past
came rushing back.

The tree was decorated on Christmas eve.
Red boots were placed on our bookcase
hoping that they would be filled
with candy, nuts and a fresh orange.

I had always put a small bell
next to my boot
as a gift for Santa.

SOLOIST II

Gently you hold
your instrument
as you begin to play.

Strong sounding notes,
blending in harmony
creating a melody
that flows freely
from your heart.

1st VALENTINE

Age seven,
with 25 cents,
I bought my first
valentine for my
mother.

Walking along the brook
I slipped and fell.
My grandfather
pulled me from the water.
I remember holding
the card safely
against my chest.

BROTHER MARION

In the shelter
of the monastery
Bro. Marion
recited his sacred vows.

Poverty, obedience, and
daily praise to God.

He was a Franciscan
at a small catholic college
in western Pennsylvania.

Bro. Marion worked in
the campus monastery
assisting the priests,
preparing the altar
for daily mass.

He often asked me to help
him carry boxes of food
from the monastery kitchen
to a car that he drove
to Altoona to visit his
sister and her family.
"Just trying to help them,
they don't have much..."

**It all seems right to me now,
food from the monastery,
Bro. Marion was feeding
the needy
in his own simple way.**

ON THE WATER

Sails unfolding
up and out
away from the mast.

Bow cutting lines
through the water
creating moving patterns
like fences
in nearby fields.

The sails hold firm into the wind.

Here on the water
my soul
is once again
renewed.

CELLIST

Holding your cello
you begin playing
the music.

As the bow moves across
the strings,
invigorating colors
come from inside your cello.

Shadows slip away,
music fills the soul,
like waters softly flowing.

A joyful feeling
as your music
wraps around you
like a winter's blanket.

Artist and cello
performing
with one voice.

GRANDMA

Over the river and through
the woods in a horse drawn sleigh
...not anymore.

Grandma drives her car
to meet grandson Dylan
and they grab lunch
at the drive-thru.

But nothing has really changed.
Grandmothers still love
their grandsons
with a tender warmth
from hearts
that never stop.

ABOUT THE AUTHOR

Born in Easton, Pennsylvania. He was raised in Oxford, New Jersey. After high school, he worked in a factory, restaurant, construction and drove a soda delivery truck. He was a member of a volunteer fire department. He received a B.A. from St. Francis College, a M.A. from Boston College. He continued his studies for a doctorate degree at SUNY/Albany.

He lives in rural upstate New York with a troupe of "found" creatures.

Printed in the United States
2377